T. W. R. SMITH.

OCT 5TH 1984

Stroud

in old picture postcards

by
Trevor A.C. Radway

European Library - Zaltbommel/Netherlands MCMLXXXIV

GB   ISBN 90 288 2817 6

European Library in Zaltbommel/Netherlands publishes among other things the following series:

IN OLD PICTURE POSTCARDS *is a series of books which sets out to show what a particular place looked like and what life was like in Victorian and Edwardian times. A book about virtually every town in the United Kingdom is to be published in this series. By the end of this year about 175 different volumes will have appeared. 1,250 books have already been published devoted to the Netherlands with the title* **In oude ansichten.** *In Germany, Austria and Switzerland 500, 60 and 15 books have been published as* **In alten Ansichten;** *in France by the name* **En cartes postales anciennes** *and in Belgium as* **En cartes postales anciennes** *and/or* **In oude prentkaarten** *150 respectively 400 volumes have been published.*

For further particulars about published or forthcoming books, apply to your bookseller or direct to the publisher.

This edition has been printed and bound by Grafisch Bedrijf De Steigerpoort in Zaltbommel/Netherlands.

FOREWORD

Stroud is an industrial town in the heart of the Cotswolds — those beautiful limestone hills which the Planners have rightly designated an area of outstanding natural beauty. Someone glibly described Stroud as a Northern mill town which had somehow strayed into rural Gloucestershire. Such a description is far less than accurate, for the woollen industry in the Stroud area predates the Roman invasion, and the tradition of its cloth manufacture owes nothing to either Lancashire or Yorkshire.

The wool of the Cotswold sheep, described by Dryden as 'living gold', made the Cotswolds rich, and the mills of the Stroud valleys spun the 'gold' into hard cash. Stroud owes its importance to being situated at the heart of five valleys, linking not only roads but also the swift running streams which were once so important to the wool trade. Only with the Industrial Revolution and the growth of the northern clothing industry did her prosperity decline. Today light industry has taken over many of the old mills, but fine woollen cloth, the 'Stroud Scarlet', prized for the manufacture of the ceremonial uniforms of the British Army, is still made in the town.

As Trevor Radway comments, the history of Stroud is indivisably linked with its neighbouring valley towns and villages, such as Nailsworth, Chalford and Stonehouse, the common factor being the wool trade. Even Painswick, 'the Queen of the Cotswolds', and regarded as one of the most perfect Cotswold villages, was once a flourishing wool town with a collection of mills along the Painswick Stream.

Mr. Radway has brought together a fascinating collection of postcards, reflecting the changing history of the Stroud area over the last eighty years. So much has altered; architecture, industry, fashion, transport, the pace of life itself, that one is tempted to think of it as a different world. Yet the changes have taken place only within a few generations, and there are still many people living who can clearly recall the scenes frozen onto the photographers' plates as the times through which they lived. Whether they were better or worse times than our own is a matter for personal preference, but the pictures brought together in this book, a vivid evocation of the past, will be a source of interest and delight to many, both young and old.

Alan Morley
Stroud Divisional Librarian

INTRODUCTION

The compilation of a book such as this presents varied problems, one of which is to achieve a balanced selection. Several worthy cards have been rejected simply because they repeated a theme in a different location. I also wished to avoid the use of photographs previously published and to the best of my knowledge I have achieved that with one exception. Which one, you can have the pleasure of finding out.

When considering the boundaries of search I had to ask myself what comprised Stroud in its broadest sense. I came to the conclusion that apart from the Town Centre many people living in the five valleys leading to Stroud would also feel such an affinity with the place to regard themselves as being in the general area of 'Stroud' especially when conversing with someone from outside the Mid-Gloucestershire area.

That decided then a pattern emerged; for the topographical description it would start in Stroud Town Centre and then follow the valleys one by one. North through Painswick to Cranham, south through Woodchester to Nailsworth, east through Brimscombe to Chalford and west through Ebley to Stonehouse. The picture content of the cards themselves had to be selected to portray the commercial, social, economic, ecological and transport mood of the area during the first quarter of the century.

Detailed close-up scenes are expected of the town centre but as one moves into the environs the distant views of, and from, hillsides are very much part of Stroud. These features have been carefully considered in my selection in an attempt to give the overall scene. It is often forgotten that one of the most important occupations in the area was, and still is, agriculture. Postcards of such a mundane subject are not common but I have managed to include a small representation.

The later pages deal with miscellaneous headings such as groups of people, transport and special events. It is inevitable that some of the cards could equally well be in one group as another. From my readings of other similar books, and book critics' views in general, it seems that postcard collectors and philatelists are also interested in the names of publishers, type of printing, country of printing, postal usage and occasional pertinent message on the back. I have tried to give details where possible without making it merely a catalogue. For those persons not conversant with the history of postcards a short comment may be useful. Generally speaking postcards printed pre-1900 in Britain are not common. Those printed prior to 1902 can often be identified by having an undivided back for writing the address only and the message, if any, was added to the photograph side. In 1902 a line was printed on the back enabling the sender to write a message on one side of the line and the address on the other. The picture would thus be unmarked.

It became fashionable to collect cards between 1902 and 1915 and many did so. Consequently the supply was increased to meet the demand, much of it with the active encouragement of the publishers. Messrs. Raphael Tuck competitions were a noteworthy example where collectors were induced to collect as many Tuck cards in a year as possible. The Post Office recorded 850 million cards of all types posted in 1908 to give you some idea of the scale of the hobby. The publishers just did not know what to print next to cater for the insatiable demand. Virtually anything that moved, or did not move, became a subject for the postcard. A good example included herein is the card of Drakes Comet in 1910. The result being no more than someone's impression of how it 'should' look. One must not decry their endeavour however, for without it we should be very much the poorer of our understanding of Edwardian Life.

The postcard was a readily available record of life close at hand when photographs in newspapers for example, were the exception rather than the rule. For a special event the photographer often took the photograph in the morning and was selling postcards of the event to bystanders in the afternoon. Private enterprise was the order of the day.

Over the years many postcards have been destroyed for various reasons. Until about 1960 they were not regarded as collectable so when someone died the collection was often burnt as being of no interest. During the war (World War II), when salvage was vital, many were turned into pulp to help the war effort. I well remember collecting waste paper on Saturday mornings during the war as my individual effort and I was personally responsible for consigning at least 500 postcards to the country's needs! There are still plenty on sale in the market place but the supply of original collections diminishes rapidly. Collectors such as myself are always anxious to see these in the hope of finding a gem. The term gem is applicable to the particular interest of the individual for there are no rules as to what is the right or wrong thing to collect. Such is the fascination of postcard collecting. Cards were collected between 1915 and 1960 but not on the scale previously stated. This was partly due to the two wars and also the depressive years in the mid-1920's and early 1930's. The majority of the postcards used in this book are from my personal collection but I must thank David Flagg of Leonard Stanley for allowing me access to his collection in order that a good coverage might be obtained. My thanks are also due to Alan Morley of Stroud for writing the introduction and reading my draft.

Trevor A.C. Radway
Painswick, Stroud

1. King Street, Stroud. This card by Hartmann shows the very imposing frontage of the Royal George Hotel in King Street. It was posted on June 25th, 1910, but was photographed somewhat earlier. It was an important hotel comparable with the Imperial Hotel near the railway station but was redeveloped as Burtons Gentlemens Outfitters in the 1930's with a Temperance Billiard Hall above. Whilst Burtons have now left, the billiard hall remains. Note the leisurely pace of the town at the time as two men and a dog stop for a chat in the centre of the road.

2745 -7.- King Street, Stroud.

King Street, Stroud.

2. King Street, Stroud. This is a very animated view so the student of costume will be able to enjoy the various styles of dress. Identifiable signs on the right are: Coley, Chemist; Tomes, Hosier; Tapper, House Furnisher, and Strange. Hepworths is on the left. Card by Walter H. Collins, Publisher, Stroud.

KING STREET, STROUD

3. King Street, Stroud, from Town Time in the 1940's. I have included this photograph to give a balanced view of the changing face of the central area. No longer do we see a policeman standing in the centre of the road to control the traffic at this point. All three streets are now 'One Way'. The direction signs to Bath were provided by the R.A.C. and below is a circular 'No Waiting' sign. The clock from which Town Time got its name is in the glass fronted alcove of Smart's Shop, which was formerly Coley's, the Chemist, and previously belonged to Robert Bragg, the Watch and Clockmaker. The time indicated was 'the standard of exact Greenwich or Railway Time... available for public use both night and day'. Town Time is now preserved in Stroud Library while a replacement clock maintains the tradition of a clock on the King Street corner. The shop on the left, next to the road signs, used to be C.B. Gardner, the Hatters and Hosiers, and was established in 1805. The window above the word 'shoes' was an original one but the next one was added when the property was sub-divided. The left side of the road is more or less original wheras much of the right side was redeveloped in 1904.

S.12926   **STROUD HIGH STREET.**

4. High Street, Stroud, from Town Time and posted in 1920, although it is probably an earlier view. There is a policeman in the street and one car outside Fosters. On the corner shop is a very fine display of lamps and also visible is the sign for W. Coward, Tailors and Outfitters, Allards Leather Shoes, W.B. Chambers, Revell and Sons Bootmakers and Abdulla Superb Cigarettes. The card is in the Kingsway Real Photo Series No. S. 12926.

12927

STROUD KING STREET.

5. King Street, Stroud, in June 1919. The car, No. AD 941, appears on the scene but barrows and horse drawn transport were still much in evidence. The luggage cart on the right is the property of the Royal George Hotel on the left. Lewis and Godfrey's shop is now the Co-op and the upper floors are very much unaltered. George Street is on the centre right. Kingsway Real Photo Series No. 12927.

STROUD, VIEW FROM GEORGE STREET.

6. George Street, Stroud, is one of the main shopping streets in the town and is depicted in this card in the Wrench Series (No. 5551) about 1905. The pony and trap is the order of the day and the card compares nicely with the next card taken in the late 1950's. In the background can be seen the corner of the Royal George Hotel, with the old buildings on the road leading off King Street Parade. The clock on the buildings on the left was a notable landmark for many years. Singer of sewing machine fame were prominent in 1905 and the shop still trades.

7. George Street in the late 1950's. The Royal George Hotel has been replaced by Burtons Outfitters, a modern structure. Beyond is the front of the Ritz Cinema, opened in 1939 and destroyed by fire in 1961. Even the cars in this scene would be much sought after by today's enthusiasts anxious to restore 'classic' vehicles.

The Subscription Rooms. Stroud.

8. The Subscription Rooms, Stroud, were built in 1832/33 at a cost of £2,500. Charles Baker of Painswick was the builder and George Basserie the Architect. The construction was financed by public subscription from local citizens in order that it might be used for public meetings. The area of fenced garden was paved completely in the 1960's. Outside the building, although not visible here, were two guns captured from Sebastopol during the Crimean War (1854). The balcony was added in 1869. A very quiet scene and vastly different from that today with its overpowering traffic intrusion.

9. Conservative Club, Stroud, the corner of Rowcroft and Russell Street at the turn of the century. The statue of George Holloway M.P. for Stroud (1886-1892) is just visible on the edge of the photo next to a poster about a Fete. He was succeeded in July 1892 by D. Brymoor Jones (Liberal) but Mr. C.A. Cripps Q.C. (Conservative) was elected in July 1895 only to be deposed again by the Liberals (C.P. Allen) in October 1900 until 1918. George Holloway (1825-1892) lived at Farm Hill (See No. 15) and was a great benefactor and employer. He originated the Mid-Gloucester Working Men's Conservative Association Benefit Society. The club later moved to George Street and then London Road.

Conservative Club, Stroud   Valentines Series   49456

10. Russell Street, Stroud, looking from the top of Rowcroft towards London Road by Walter Collins of Stroud. Russell Street was constructed during the 1860's when the town centre was expanded. Access to the Great Western Station was thus improved. The station was built by the Cheltenham and Great Western Union Railway and opened in 1845 on land known as 'Great Shurmers'. The large building behind the gas lamp is the General Post Office, opened in 1885 having moved from George Street. The former George Street building became the 'Post Office Inn' and is now closed. Lewis and Godfrey's shop on the left was one of the largest in Stroud, formerly fronting onto King Street it expanded into Russell Street in 1896 and was ideally located to serve passengers by train or on the buses using King Street. It later became the Co-op.

STD-22 STROUD, Russell Street.

11. Russell Street, Stroud, has seen many changes in the last twenty years and it is surprising how the changing scene is not really noticed until one looks back at a photograph such as this. Steel's Garage and adjoining buildings have been demolished to be replaced by offices and a supermarket and several other buildings have had their fenestration drastically changed. Even the street furniture changes, the rectangular 'No Entry' sign beside Simms Clock is no more. The clock itself was built in 1921 as the result of a bequest by Thomas Simms of Uplands who died in 1917. Mr. Simms was a wine and spirits merchant in the town and very much involved in local politics. The double deck bus is in a two tone livery, possibly red and white when this photograph was taken in the late-1950's by Friths.

The Uplands, Stroud

12. Uplands, Stroud. This area was developed as a residential area between 1850 and 1900 and the photograph shows Slad Road running left to right at the bottom, with Springfield Road at the higher level. In the valley floor alongside Slad Brook are small factories. The frontage to Landsdown Road has also been infilled at the beginning of the century. The card was posted in Stroud on December 15th, 1906, and was printed by Geo. H. James & Co. of Stroud.

13. The Parish Church, Stroud, in 1878 reproduced on a card posted in May 1905. It shows the restoration of the spire after being struck by lightning. It states 'While this photograph was being taken, W. Cheriton, a member of the choir, stood on the highest point of the spire balancing on one leg — a remarkable exhibition of strong nerves and coolness', one might add stupidity as well!

THE PARISH CHURCH, STROUD, during restoration of spire, after having been struck by lightning, March 1878. (From an old photo.)

While this photograph was being taken, W. Cheriton, a member of the choir, stood on the highest point of the spire, balancing upon one leg—a remarkable exhibition of strong nerve and coolness.

BURROW, PUBLISHER, CHELTENHAM

Beeches Green, Stroud.

14. Stroud, a view of Beeches Green Road in 1921 looking towards Painswick. Considerable road improvements were carried out in the early 1960's and again in 1976 when the wall and gateway to St. Rose's Convent on the left were altered. The Magistrates' Court and Police Station on the right were blighted by an attempt to build an Inner Ring Road through the town, only abandoned after a Public Enquiry in 1976, but still exist with a new occupier. The pony and trap descending the hill was probably bringing a middle class lady into Stroud from the country. A real photo by Walter A. Collins, Publisher, Stroud.

Memorial Arch, Farmhill Park, Stroud

15. Memorial Arch, Farmhill Park, Paganhill, posted in October 1918. The archway was 'Erected... to commemorate the abolition of Slavery in the British Colonies 1 August 1834'. It was built by Henry Wyatt, owner of a mansion called Farm Hill, and spanned the entrance to that house. The house itself has been demolished leaving only its name in Farmhill Estate. The arch was refurbished by the Stroud Urban District Council in 1961. The wall on the left survives but a housing estate road leading to Archway School now passes to the right of the arch.

The maypole
Paganhill

16. The Maypole, Paganhill. There has been a maypole at Paganhill since time immemorial. At times it would be taken down for repainting then re-erected by the local men, in itself a ceremony. There are fourteen in shirt sleeves in this photograph and all of them would have been needed to erect the pole which is at least 100 feet high. Maypoles were partly devoted to fertility rites and maypoles with their attendant rituals still survive today. 1st May was formerly celebrated throughout Britain and to a lesser extent in France and Germany with festivities which now survive only in rural areas. A May Queen was crowned and people danced around the Maypole which was decorated with flowers and ribbons. Maypoles were forbidden to be erected by the Roundhead Parliament in 1644 but were later allowed in the Restoration period. 'Fisher' states, an accident here in 1804 killed two children.

RUSCOMBE Nr STROUD

17. Ruscombe near Stroud. The Chapel has been removed and only one or two foundation stones can be seen today. The roadway, known as Sion Hill, leading to the Chapel is one of the steepest in the district being about 1 in 3 and must have deterred all but the most dedicated of worshippers. The quarry face was the source of the stone used locally for walling. Many of the cottages survive in their original form in this pleasant sun trap some 350 feet above Stroud. At one time Whiteshill and Ruscombe 'exhibited a very low type and a very degraded state of social and moral life'. It had a reputation for supplying all the beggars in the district. This deplorable state of affairs was ameliorated by the formation of a Chapel of Independent Dissentors at Ruscombe and by other religious and educational processes.

18. This marvellous real photograph of circa 1905 shows a group of school children outside Painswick School on Stroud Road. The school, on the left of the picture, was opened in 1846 and was a National School owned by the Church Commissioners. Practically every boy is wearing a cap and all the girls have regulation black stockings. Notice the fine Cotswold stone wall and the gas lamp. The stone probably came by horse and cart from the local Catbrain Quarry on Painswick Beacon. The village car park is now located behind the wall on the right of the picture.

THE YEWS. PAINSWICK CHURCHYARD. 1148.

19. Painswick Churchyard. This card was posted in October 1930 and is an interesting and unusual view of the Churchyard. It was taken from the Temperance Hotel (now a house) beside the Town Hall, see card No. 20. It shows the magnificent yew trees of which there are reputed to be ninety-nine, the hundredth, it is said, will not grow. The War Memorial is surrounded by railings which formed a barrier. Some of the ancient, and much admired, tombs and vaults can be seen on the left of the photograph. A lamp was erected in 1904, just off the right of the photograph, 'to celebrate the completion of the 60th year of the reign of Queen Victoria'. Later is was resited on top of the wall near the telegraph pole. The GWR bus, with luggage rack on top and steps at the rear, stands opposite The Falcon Hotel. Mr. Tidmarsh's butchers shop was next door, behind the bus. The AA sign high on the wall of The Falcon acknowledges the more general use of motor cars although the scene is very tranquil by today's standards.

20. Painswick Town Hall. The exact date or purpose of this gathering is not known but I think it is circa 1899. The Highways Act of 1835 imposed on the Surveyor of Highways the duty to discharge the Common Law liability of the inhabitants at large, of a parish, to repair the highways within it. The man in the bowler hat and spats could be the Surveyor and the mixed bunch armed with a brush, seven hoes, five scrapers and a rake could be the workforce engaged upon minor repairs and cleaning. Who was the man with the bell? A man with a notepad is next to the soldier and everyone wears a cap. Behind the group is the Temperance Hotel and Painswick Coffee Tavern from which photograph No. 19 was taken. The price list is fixed on the ironwork porch with a pagoda top similar to that at Ebley Halt (No. 62). Painswick Post Office is in the background with a gas lamp on the wall.

21. Painswick Postmen. This card is of particular personal interest as it was shown to me as a result of my research into the card of Swan Lane, Stroud (No. 57). Charlie West stands beside the bicycle on which he delivered the mail twice a day to Cranham Village. Edwin Durham West, owner of the horse and trap, is on the far right. The bicycle has thick blow up tyres and a carbide lamp. Behind the bicycle is an Army Recruiting Poster and Provost Oats are displayed in the shop window. Some of the cards to be seen on the board on the wall are described in this book. Date is about 1918-1920. This was the original Painswick Post Office which is now the Painswick Bakery, the Post Office having moved up the street about 25 yards in 1934.

Friday Street
Painswick

22. Friday Street, Painswick. The message on this card says 'Just a peep at one of the old streets in Painswick' and was posted in 1927. The village, being long established at this time, had several similarly old streets. The cobbled footway was one of the last to survive in Painswick and they are today, sadly, all tarpaved. The Bell Inn sold Smith and Sons Fine Brimscombe Ales and Stout and later Godsells Fine Ales. It was demolished in 1941 subsequent to damage by German bombs. The bombing took place as an isolated incident on just one night and it is thought that nine bombs fell on the village. Two persons were killed by the bombs, both evacuees from the south-east coast. A 79-year old man died in Friday Street and Mrs. Ruby Heaton-Watson (51) in another house on the outskirts of the village. The Bell Inn was in existence pre-1840 and the street was formerly known as Bell Street. It is not known why and when it became Friday Street. Beyond The Bell was a slaughterhouse owned by Mr. Webb who had a butchers shop opposite. The site is now occupied by the Catholic Church.

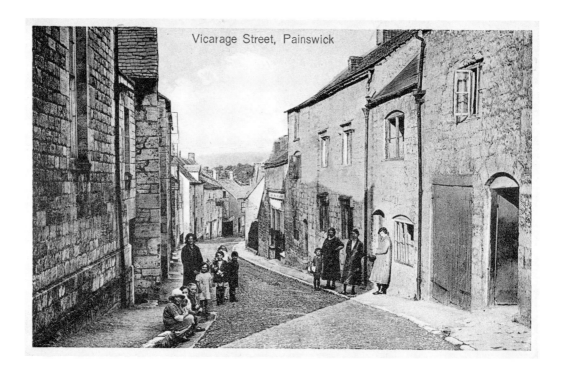

Vicarage Street, Painswick

23. The visit of a photographer to Vicarage Street, Painswick, was obviously of great interest to some of the locals. Identified in the group are Edith and Mary Staite, Mrs. Staite and Mrs. Barnard. This was essentially a village street of artisan housing interspersed with one or two fine residences and it has always been very much at the 'heart' of Painswick. There was a time when the top end of the street was considered to be distinctly 'rough'. The White Horse Inn, nicknamed The Pony, can be seen in the centre background and a shop which ended its days as a Greengrocer/Fish Shop can be seen on the right. Local stone has been used in the buildings and the windows reflect the influence of local mills in their style.

Parkwall-Cranham Woods.

24. This card of Parkwall, Cranham, epitomises a rural Gloucestershire scene in the late 1920's. The road which even then was a major route is seen to be little more than a country lane by today's standards. It was opened as a Turnpike Road in 1820 and is now part of the Bath to Cheltenham principal route. The common land on the right of the picture is crossed by rough stone tracks which have long since been surfaced. Trees have grown up close to the road giving a 'closed in' appearance. The cottage on the right has a thatched roof now replaced by tiles requiring much less maintenance. The horse is standing at the junction of Port Way which leads to Gloucester and in the middle background is the Lodge House to Prinknash Abbey. The card was printed by The Cotswold Publishing Company of Wotton under Edge, Gloucestershire.

Cranham Village

25. Cranham Village nestles amongst the hills at the tip of the Stroud district. This view, posted on 22 December 1924, records the quiet life of a truly rural Cotswold scene. A hayrick has been built right in the centre of the village and the high standard of cultivation is evident. At the foot of the hill a horse and cart wait near a shed. Some properties have been demolished and new infilling has taken place in the last thirty years. This card was published by Spring of Painswick and printed at the Cotswold Publishing Co. in Wotton under Edge.

THE NEW INN. SELSLEY COMMON. 3833.

26. The New Inn, Selsley, in the 1930's. The road to Dursley passes across the centre of the photograph. The open air skittle alley was a feature of this public house and the game is still as popular as ever in Gloucestershire, albeit inside. The building is now completely demolished and the site area is included in the extensive Selsley Common. Note the large flag pole on the left. The signs on the building advertise that it was fully licensed and sold Stroud Ales.

27. Rodborough Fort, Stroud. Whilst this card is of no great topographical interest it is quite remarkable for its artistic qualities. So many of the postcards illustrated in this book do not really exploit the pictorial possibilities. This was produced by Walter Collins of High Street, Stroud, and was used as the basis for a similar card of a painting by A.R. Quinton, a well known illustrator of the period.

Rodborough Fort, Stroud.

AMBERLEY NEAR STROUD.

28. Amberley. There are many cards of this village but this one can be considered at the heart of the place in that The Amberley Inn is on the left of the photograph. This view, posted on July 24, 1907, is in the F. Hartmann Real Glossy Series G 2745/23. Looking towards Littleworth, the drinking fountain and guide post are prominent behind the children on the road. The relative importance of Amberley, photographically speaking, was due entirely to the association with Rose Cottage (where the novel John Halifax, Gentleman, was partly written).

29. Dunkirk Mills in the late 1890's. The mills used to manufacture walking sticks etcetera. The footpath in the foreground leads from Lower Forest Green, across the main Bath Road and right into the Mill Yard, thus making for easy access for the workers. The Nailsworth Brook, with its abundant water supply ran to the rear of the buildings. Pinfarthings is in the right background. Dunkirk Mills were referred to in Mrs. Craik's novel John Halifax, Gentleman, also connected with Tewkesbury (which was used as the setting for her characters). At one time the novel gained much local publicity but with a wider set of values and interest in the 1920's the public gradually forgot it. Postcard by E. & A. Conway of Nailsworth.

Nailsworth

30. This card, published by M.H. Redman, Stationer, of Nailsworth, is in the MM Series (No. 50661) printed in Germany. It dates about 1901-02 and shows the buildings in the Railway Yard in the foreground with the Railway Hotel and Bridge Street. The photograph was taken from Watledge almost exactly opposite view No. 31. St. George's Church, the large building in the centre, dominates Fountain Street and beyond it Bath Road climbs southwards. Development took place at the rear of the church in the 1920's and 1930's. Spring Hill, leading to Forest Green, climbs to the right.

Watledge, Nailsworth, near Stroud

31. Watledge, Nailsworth. This attractive view shows the Midland Railway Goods Yard off Bridge Street. This was the terminus of the Stonehouse to Nailsworth Branch line. The bridge over the river was maintained by the Railway Company and a cast iron notice 'by order of John Williams 1899' is fixed to the wall. Two railwaymen stand opposite the gas lamp and behind them, and the tree, is the Railway Hotel. The yard on the left contained some very nice red brick buildings one of which survives. The station itself was at a higher level and reached by a footpath to the left of the gate in the middle distance. The houses in Watledge, as the name suggests, sit on a ledge in the steep hillside and formed a complete enclave with their own public house. Smith Volume 1 however, says that the name is from 'Wattle hedge'. The card was posted on October 30th, 1906.

Fountain Street, Nailsworth, near Stroud

32. Fountain Street, Nailsworth, which gained its name from the drinking fountain located near the spire in the centre of the photograph. A carriage with two horses stands outside Jefferys Domestic Supply, Cycle and Motor Works. The outbuildings at the rear of the George Hotel are on the right and Bridge Street extends into the middle distance. The fountain is now sited in Old Market near the bus station. Valentine Series No. 49468.

33. Hillier of Nailsworth displays a shop front typical of the period. The 'standard' shop front of this type has largely disappeared from many British towns mainly as the result of redevelopment schemes in the 1960's when multiples moved into the towns and required a modern fenestration more suitable to display their wares. The twenty-four panes of glass on each side of the doorway required labour intensive cleaning and were dated. Stroud and some of the villages in the district are fortunate in that some examples similar to this still survive. Many of them are 'listed' as being of architectural importance and for that we must be thankful, even if the owners of the properties concerned consider it to be something of a burden.

A Bit of
Old Nailsworth

near Stroud

34. This vignette view of the Red Lion, Nailsworth, looking from Market Street towards Bath Raod portrays a real bit of old Nailsworth. The Red Lion Inn offers Dewars Perth Whisky or Martells Three Star Brandy. Just to the right was Nailsworth Brewery making less expensive brews. There is a fine gas lamp on the corner of Simmond's shop from where the lady is watching an elderly man brushing the street.

The Golden Valley.   *Stroud.*

35. The Golden Valley, as the valley east of Stroud is known, was the source of employment for many in 1909. The mills were situated alongside the water supply, the River Frome, within easy reach of transport in the form of the Thames and Severn Canal and the Great Western Railway yards at both Stroud and Brimscombe from 1845 on. Nowadays most of the manufactured goods are carried along the A419 road through the valley. The mills produced a wide range of goods from walking sticks, pins and needles to cloth. Note how the housing was beginning to spread up the hillsides. The mill on the left is Griffin's Mill and the one just left of centre is Ham Mills. The building in the right centre is shown as a school (Butter Row) on the 1902 Ordnance Survey Map.

36. The Cross, Minchinhampton, looking from West End past High Street and up Tetbury Street. The population of this ancient parish in 1914 was 3,702. Minchinhampton is a good example of the use of Oolitic Limestone by local masons. Even the humblest of cottages were built of stone quarried just down the road. Communications were a problem due to the elevated position of the village so it was very advantageous to use local materials which also included stone tiles for the roofs. These are very heavy and require a steeply pitched roof to support them. This photograph typifies this architectural style complete with dormer windows into the roof space thus making additional rooms. Ices and teas were available from the corner shop or you could fill up with paraffin from the pump. The Salutation Inn for Stroud Ales and Stout is in the centre.

Brimscombe, Basin.

37. Brimscombe Basin. Frank Cooper's house, Brimscombe Terrace, No. 38, can be seen left of centre. This quite large 'port' is well portrayed here. The waterside cottages were occupied by the canal maintenance men and other buildings were used for storage and warehousing purposes. Slightly to the right of this view was the boatbuilding yard of Abdela and Mitchell Ltd. of Hope Mill. A wide range of vessels were built here and shipped down the Thames and Severn and Stroudwater Canals to the Severn and distant purchasers. The road to Minchinhampton Common rises above the port and most of the intervening land has now been built on. Wrench Series No. 15737, circa 1905.

38. 'A corner of Brimscombe Port' postmarked 1904. The boat is 'Gem' of Gloster possibly owned by Jones & Martin of Chalford. Being about 10 feet or 12 feet in the beam this would be the head of navigation for such a craft. The buildings in the background were formerly called Brimscombe Terrace but now known as Terrace House. The River Frome flows between the gates and the house but today the gates have gone. The attractive Victorian porch can still be seen. Frank Cooper advertised that he was a plumber, glazier, painter, paper hanger, gas and hot water fitter and house decorator. A useful chap to know! The Basin is now Bensons car park but all the buildings still exist.

Chalford.   Stroud.

39. Ballinger's Lock, Chalford, on the Thames and Severn Canal which was constructed in the Stroud Valley between 1780-1790. In the centre can be seen the Chalford Round House built about 1783 as a watch tower for lock keepers. It was built in a circular form based on a style of old wool drying towers. The lock keeper also had to look after the towpaths etcetera. The canal brought coal and raw materials into the Stroud Valley from the Forest of Dean and Staffordshire. To the right of The Round House is The Company's Arms Inn (so named after its association with the East India Company), a building of Elizabethan origin built on the site of a Coaching House and known to date back to about 1300 A.D.

CHALFORD

40. Grist Mill Lock, Chalford, published by F. Major of Bisley, a notable recorder of many local scenes. Ballinger's Lock can be seen below the bridge and the road behind the photographer led down to Iles's Mill and to Burleigh. The photograph was taken about 1915 and shows the Thames and Severn Canal in good working order. The winding gear on the lockgate is well kept and appears to have been renewed in 1908. It will be seen from the size of the lock that two boats could be taken through at each lift. The constriction of the Chalford Valley is apparent here and only 200 yards west is the very narrowest part where the road, canal, railway and River Frome squeezed through on the north slope of the valley. The buildings are often two storey on one side and three storey on the other due to the severe slope of the land.

London Road, Chalford (3)

41. Looking west along the London Road Chalford in Edwardian days. The card was published by Tomkins and Barrett of Swindon in the 'Famous Series' and posted in Chalford on 11 May 1914. London Road became a Turnpike Road in 1814 with a Toll House near Christ Church. The Turnpike Trusts were local bodies who had the power to levy tolls on users of the highway under their control, applying the money raised to maintainance and improvement of the roads. The Turnpike was the gate with its tollhouse and keeper where payment had to be made on every vehicle or animal entering the next section of road. The last road tolls were in 1895. The gentleman with the donkey equipped with panniers is prepared for a haul up the very narrow paths which serve as the only means of access to a good many houses in Chalford.

42. High Street, Central Stores and Post Office, Chalford. Published by F.C. Smart, The Golden Valley Supply Stores, Chalford in the Vulcan Series. It was commonplace in the Victorian and Edwardian eras to paint advertisements on the facades of buildings. This is an excellent example of the art although one may argue that the plethora of information detracts from the impact of any particular sign. Most of the wording can be easily read so I will not elaborate. Sadly none of it is visible today as the rendering has been painted over.

CHALFORD. THE LOCKS.

43. Bell Lock, Chalford. To complete the Chalford sequence is Bell Lock just to the east of the Turnpike Road from where the photograph was taken. The Bell Inn itself faces onto High Street, Chalford and the New Red Lion is at right angles to High Street. The steep paths referred to in No. 41 can be seen on the hillside above High Street. The River Frome cannot be seen on this photograph but it flows between the Canal and the Bell Inn. The Thames and Severn Canal was established by an Act of Parliament in 1783. It passed to Gloucestershire County Council in 1901 in a state of decline as a commercial waterway, culminating in its final abandonment in 1933. Isolated sections still exist but the aspirations of local preservationists appear to be unrealistic when one considers the development which has taken place on many parts of the former canal.

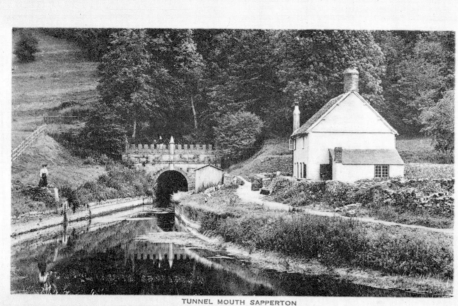

TUNNEL MOUTH SAPPERTON

44. Sapperton Tunnel is nearly 2¼ miles in length and took five years to construct. It has a Gothic portal at one end and a Classic style portal at the other. It was opened in 1789 and closed in 1927, the last working boat using it in 1911. Boats were propelled through the tunnel by men lying on their backs on the boats and 'walking' along the walls or roof. There was always a chronic shortage of water on this section as the tunnel is on the highest part of the canal and much water was also needed for the flight of locks down to Chalford. Clay puddling and concrete lining were required to keep the water in the canal. The cottage was probably habitated by a Thames and Severn Canal employee. Behind the photographer was the Daneway Inn which had wharfage and accommodation for overnight stops. It was probably still called the Bricklayers' Arms at this time. Card published by F. Major of Bisley.

45. Cainscross, Stroud. A postcard by F. Major of Bisley showing the 'White Horse Inn' on the left with a direction sign to Stonehouse and Gloucester on the wall. The traveller turned right for Nailsworth and Bath and straight on for Stroud centre. The large white building in the centre was removed for major road works in the mid-1960's and the wide road is now flanked by Tricorn House. The gable-ended building on the left is Cainscross Post Office.

46. The Canal at Ebley. Ebley Mills were one of the largest in the area and were used for the manufacture of woollen cloth. They are viewed here from the edge of Dudbridge. A swingbridge over the canal linked the Mills to the Main Road in Ebley (No. 47). This section of canal was known as Stroudwater Navigation (1789) and permitted navigation from the River Severn, and later the Sharpness Canal, at Framilode, to Stroud where it linked to the Thames and Severn Canal and eventually the River Thames at Lechlade. The Canal continued until 1954 and has largely been filled in at this point. There have been efforts to restore it since 1972. The mill is now used as a printing works. Card by W.D.M. & Co. of Cirencester in the 'Cecily' Series.

Ebley, Stroud.

G. Olpin, Post Office, Ebley.

47. Main Road, Ebley. Apart from the mode of transport there is much similarity to be seen between today's view and this one, dated August 1905, produced by Burrow of Cheltenham. The buildings on the left were a bacon factory at this time with a laundry adjoining. Just off the picture on the right was an abbatoir. There is much local pressure today to build a bypass for this section of road.

CAINSCROSS BREWERY

48. Cainscross Brewery on a card posted on June 3rd, 1912. At one time most towns had small independent breweries all competing for trade but slowly they became absorbed by larger firms and today we have a very limited choice of beer. Stroud was no exception. Stroud Brewery bought out many small firms and closed down the old brewery buildings, only to be absorbed by West Country Brewery and later by Whitbread. This brewery, formerly owned by Carpenter and Co., is now used by an Agricultural Merchant and the chimneys have long gone but the main building with the clerestory lights still exists. The River Frome was an important source of water and ran under the Brewery as it still does. The card is in the 'Stroud News Series' and the message refers to 'having a nice tea and band on Empire Day'. The Brewery was at one time connected by rail to the Stonehouse to Nailsworth Branch of the Midland Railway.

49. Pearcroft Road, Stonehouse. This card was posted in Stonehouse in December 1906 and was photographed by F. Restall of Stonehouse. It shows a rank of houses which were quite new at the time. The group of children on the grass found the photographer of great interest and are not concerned with the horse and cart which had been posed to add interest. The name on the front of the cart is not clear but the owner would have been a local farmer or tradesman. This card was printed in black and white with colour tint added on the larger surfaces. Stonehouse Brick and Tile Works were situated to the rear of the houses and it is more than likely that the house bricks came from there.

50. Regent Street, Stonehouse, by H. Lockyear Photos, Stonehouse. Fourteen people take an airy ride from outside the Nagshead Inn which sold Godsell and Sons Fine Ales. It was a Family and Commercial Posting House run by Mr. and Mrs. Branches with Good Stabling. A.W. Ford was the Proprietor. Alfred Ford was also a licensed retailer of beer porter and cider. The premises were not shown as a public house on the 1920 map.

WHILEY.

LOWER HIGH STREET, STONEHOUSE.

51. Lower High Street, Stonehouse. Card No. 554 published by Mark Whiley, Stationer, Stonehouse, and posted on November 11, 1905. His premises are shown on the right centre next to Blick the Ironmonger. The lad pushing the large wheeled handcart feels it is time for a rest. Horse droppings on the carriageway presented a major problem for those attempting to keep the streets clean. Throughout the country it resulted in a manure problem of millions of tons per year which only disappeared when motor cars became commonplace in the later part of this century.

Stonehouse.

The Crown and Anchor Hotel.

The Wrench Series, No 3443

52. The Crown and Anchor Hotel, Stonehouse, on a card posted on January 29th, 1906. It was produced in the Wrench Series (No. 3443) and was printed in Saxony. The large building is set well back from the road with wide grass separation giving the village green feeling. The carriages parked outside indicate its popularity and importance. Stabling was available at the rear. The large building on the right was the Post Office which has now moved further up the street. On the verge is a stone milestone and the roadway itself, with loose surface, show signs of the passage of vehicles.

Stonehouse.

Upper High Street.

53. Upper High Street, Stonehouse. The Crown and Anchor Inn is on the left of this photograph (see No. 52) which gives a very good overall view of the street about 1910. Many of the buildings survive today although the shop fronts have changed considerably. This group of children are posed for the photograph and they have no concern for traffic which is evidently mostly horse drawn.

GEORGE HOTEL. FROCESTER.

54. George Hotel, Frocester. Photographer Frederick Restall of Stonehouse got out and about to take this photograph post-marked 1906 in Frocester. The public house located at a crossroads has always been a stopping off point. The signpost on the right points to Frocester Station (about a mile) closed as a result of the Beeching Axe in the 1960's. The iron fence around the tree was probably erected to prevent animals from chewing the bark of the tree and has long since been removed. Many fences of this type were removed in the Second World War to provide munitions. Behind the fence is an old wooden wheelbarrow, very heavy even when empty. The George has been renamed The Royal Gloucestershire Hussar. Just discernable in the distance is a horse and cart standing outside the village smithy. By the end of last century the blacksmith was essential in maintaining farm machinery and transport as well as his role as a farrier. He would also make wrought iron gates, chains and tools of all kinds. By 1900 he was also becoming a motor mechanic primarily because he was the one man in a village who could be expected to understand machinery.

55. The Champion motorcycle as supplied by Miles of Berkeley and Sharpness. It was fitted with a Jap engine and transmission to the back wheel was by a friction belt which must have resulted in lack of traction in wet weather. The riding position was very upright with long handlebars and a well sprung saddle to compensate for the poor roads. The early motorcycles were a development of a basic pedal cycle frame on which an engine and controls etc. were hung. They were often crude, unreliable, and developed little power. They were single geared without any clutch and had poor brakes. The chain drive gave more positive transmission when it was first introduced in 1901. The pedals on this particular model gave the opportunity of manual assistance on hills. AD 1306 was registered in Gloucestershire just after the turn of the century.

56. The proud owner of this motorcycle combination, registered number AD 4144, was really dressed for the occasion in his breeches and boots. The flat cap was almost a standard issue for young and old alike. Notice the acetyline lamps and the well upholstered sidecar. In 1905 there were great technical advancements in motorcycles and by 1913 there were about 150,000 on the roads of Britain. The road surface here was remarkably good for a country district where water bound aggregate sealed with tarspray was the norm. The postcard was published by K. Ltd.

57. Swan Lane, Stroud, showing the Swan Inn and a very elegant gentleman on his pony and trap. The plaque above the wheel says West, Painswick, Glos. The 1835 Highways Act, S.76, required that names and place of abode of owners be painted on all wagons (offside) carts etc. to be used on the highway. The person here was Edwin Durham West, a postman of Painswick, who used to deliver in Holcombe by bicycle. The pony and trap were his own which he kept at the back of his house in Gloucester Street, Painswick.

58. The Grove, Chalford, with the Great Western Railway bus waiting to take passengers to Stroud Station via Brimscombe. The GWR began the service in 1905 and it was merged with the Western National Company in 1929. This bus, number CO 84, was first registered in Plymouth whereas other similar buses were registered in London (A) and Cornwall (AF). The conductor with his leather money bag leans against the bus and the driver has some female companionship. The tyres are solid rubber, not much better than wagon wheels. An outside stairway at the back leads to the upper level for those wanting to sample fresh air and uninterrupted views. Photographed by H.M.C.

59. Chalford Station, showing a spare Push and Pull coach awaiting a duty. Behind it horses haul away goods from the wagons. Items of railway interest are the gas lamps and the loading gauge near the coach. There is also a hand operated crane in the yard. The bridge carrying the road on the left had recently been rebuilt. The Thames and Severn Canal is at the foot of the embankment and the rear of the Bell Inn in High Street can also be seen.

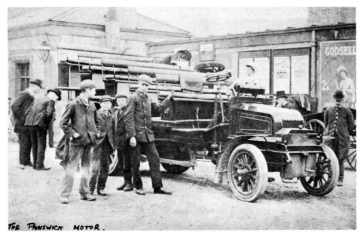

THE PAINSWICK MOTOR.

60. Above: The Painswick Motor outside Stroud Station. There were two stations in Stroud, this one built in stone by the Cheltenham & Great Western Union Railway in 1845 and the other about 150 yards due south built by the Midland Railway as a spur to the Stonehouse & Nailsworth Railway in 1886. That station was a timber structure and was known as Stroud Cheapside. The GWR buses were generally covered vehicles whereas this is an open topped type. Note the advertisement for Godsells Imperial Ales at 2/6 and 1/6 and the poster relating to the England-Ireland Ferry Route operated by the GWR via Fishguard. The bus registration is A 6048 and is obviously interesting to the spectators. W.F. Lee Photographic Series. Below: The London and South Western Railway lent the Great Western Railway its new Steam Rail Car in October 1902 for trials between Stroud and Chalford. The GWR liked the idea and began running its first car between Stroud and Chalford on 12th October 1903. New Halts were opened with notices pointing to 'GWR Rail Motor Platform'. The first cars were 57 feet long and had 3 feet 8 inches driving wheels and direct drive. They were fifty-two seaters and were gas lit. The conversion of GWR Steam Cars to trailer coaches, i.e. hauled by a locomotive, began in 1917 and continued until 1935 when the last car was withdrawn from service. This view shows No. 6 in Stroud GWR Station in June 1906. The end towards the camera is that of the guard, the driver and fireman being at the other end. The chimney is just visible on the roof.

The Motor Ebley Crossing, Stroud

EBLEY CROSSING
HALTE

61. Railmotor No. 50, a 70 feet car, stands at Ebley Crossing Halte (note the spelling) near Chapel Lane, with a Chalford to Gloucester local train. The Railmotors were fitted with steps which allowed persons to mount or dismount even when the platform was very short or even at level crossings if necessary. A typical Great Western 'Pagoda' building can be seen on the platform constructed of old railway sleepers. The later steam engine and trailer cars formed an important part of the area's transport for almost sixty years when it was sadly withdrawn by British Railways on 29th November 1964. Two preserved railcars can still be seen on the Dean Forest Railway at Lydney. Valentine Series card posted on December 8th, 1906.

62. Haresfield Station (Midland Railway) looking south. The card was posted at Stonehouse on June 11th, 1907. There were four tracks at Haresfield at this time, those shown being the Midland. On the extreme left can be seen a tall signal which controlled trains on the Great Western Railway. It was a frequent occurrence on this joint section between Standish Junction and Tuffley Junction for trains belonging to the two rival Companies to race each other. At one or other of the junctions they each went their separate ways. A level crossing can be seen in front of the signal box. This box controlled the crossing of all four tracks. The buildings are typical timber construction of the Midland Railway and the large staff of eight are lined up on the platform for their photograph. Note the machine dispensing Nestlés chocolate just in front of the smaller building. The platforms are made of timber and near the crossing an old van body without wheels acts as a store.

THE RUINS OF STATION HOUSE,
AFTER THE FIRE. (S) HARESFIELD 1911.

63. Haresfield Station, the ruins of the Stationmaster's house, posted on 31st August 1908. It is interesting to note the (s) after the word fire, implying that there had been more than one. The Midland Railway porter looks rather forlorn. Thatch cottages were fairly common in the Severn Vale and this one probably predated the coming of the Railway in 1844. Surprisingly the message on the back of the card makes no reference to the fire. The frequent horror of fire in thatch roofs was always a problem and primitive fire fighting equipment was sometimes kept in a central location such as the Parish Church. This included hooks and grappling irons for dragging down the blazing thatch before the rest of the structure caught alight. Thatch was generally selected wheat straw with a roof life of fifteen-twenty years. As tiles and slates became more readily available, the use of thatch declined and today is the exception rather than the rule.

64. Bisley. This card, which states Hawkley, Bisley, on the back, typifies the rural scene one would find in Gloucestershire right up to the Second World War. By the end of 1875 about 40,000 Mc Cormick type reapers (from U.S.A.) were in use in Britain and a two horse reaper could cut as much corn in an hour as the best labourer could cut by hand in a day. They cut and delivered the crop in a way which made it easy to gather and bind into sheaves secured with a straw band. On steep gradients around Stroud it was often necessary to use two horses and was a convenient method of making hay etcetera, in small fields prior to the introduction of tractor towed combines and balers.

Carting home the Corn.

The Wrench Series, No. 6804

65. Carting home the Corn, in the Wrench Series (No. 6804) shows how labour intensive the harvest used to be. After cutting, the bundles of corn were placed in stooks, allowed to dry, then manhandled onto a cart for transportation to a barn or farmyard rick where it was subsequently thrashed. This involved a pitcher, a loader and a carter. The loading was an expert job as the load had to be secure enough for its passage over rough ground, the higher it got the greater the possibility of disaster. The general purpose wooden farmcart would be locally made including the wheels at a wheelwright's shop. Nowadays the Combine Harvester works all through the day, and much of the night, cutting and thrashing and throwing out the stalks etcetera at the rear. Such is progress. The farmworkers are smartly dressed in collarless shirts but with waistcoats and of course, caps. Cotswold Photographer Percy Simms specialised in this type of scene.

66. Building the Rick, thought to be Leonard Stanley, about 1905. Prior to the advent of the baler and elevator the building of the hayrick, or strawrick, was arduous and labour intensive. The men weilding the pitchforks would need their hats to keep the flies at bay on a hot day. The long and stout wooden ladder on the left was very necessary when rickbuilding. Today we see fork lift equipment on the front of tractors stacking the box-like bales. The top of the stack was pitched and thatched with straw to keep out the weather. The rick would inevitably subside under its own weight and internal heat. The heat would sometimes lead to spontaneous combustion so the rick had to be temperature tested at regular intervals by thrusting a long metal probe into the rick for a few minutes then assessing the 'feel' of the iron. On occasion it had to be partially demolished to allow it to cool.

67. Elementary School. Whilst this school cannot be positively identified, it is in the Stroud area. It was found in a collection of 'local' cards. The austere wooden desks with little or no space for books are far removed from the modern classroom. Heating would have been from a large coke or coal stove tended by the teacher. The walls do not lend themselves to visual display material and the globe is given great prominence. The children are well dressed and are dressed uniformly apart from the sailor suit. One can only postulate whether the Schools Inspector was expected. The desks at the back of the class appear to be two tier possibly for bigger children. The high window sill prevents distraction from outside sources and the general air is severe, instilling timidity in the children.

68. On Thursday July 16th, 1924, Stroud Hospital held a Carnival. Rodborough Infants School entered a float called 'Nursery-land'. The cart itself was well painted and every endeavour was made to disguise it with paintings along its sides. Mary and her Lamb, Humpty Dumpty and Jack and Jill are easily identifiable. It was obviously a big day for the children some of whom may still be in the area, albeit a little longer in the tooth.

69. Eastington Band of Hope Picnic Party, 1907. A splendid galaxy of Edwardian dress, most of the men sport beards like the King's and large floral hats were the thing for the ladies. The man in the centre with the jug looks happy enough, confirmation of the contents would be interesting but it would almost certainly be tea or orange juice as the Band of Hope were a Temperance movement. The reverend gentleman typifies the ideal of the late Victorian style of preachers.

MME FLORENCE, THE GLOBE-WALKER, IN STROUD.

70. Mademoiselle Florence, The Globewalker, at the top of Russell Street about 1910. I am unable to describe the feat in detail or the reason for it but she can be clearly seen standing on a ball midst a large audience. Speculate for yourself just what she was trying to achieve. Whilst it is not well focused it is a most interesting and I suspect rare card photographed by W.F. Lee. The notice on the board appears to be in French. I understand a number of circuses visited the Subscription Rooms at the turn of the century and she may have been one of the attractions doing a publicity preview.

RODBORO MANOR after fire
Aug. 29

H.J.Camley
PHOTO

71. This postcard of Rodborough Manor after a fire is quite clearly dated August 1929 and photographed by H.J. Camley. I make this point because I have seen a similar photograph, although taken from a different angle, quite clearly postmarked 28th August 1906. The extent of the damage is identical especially above the lintels. I can only surmise that there were two fires and that Mr. Camley simply resurrected the old photograph, added the date, 1929, and sold the postcards. Anyone who fancies a little research could pursue the matter possibly by reference to newspaper reports of the periods in question. Disaster cards are scarce, interesting and sought after as they often recorded an event in the district which at the time was important but subsequently forgotten.

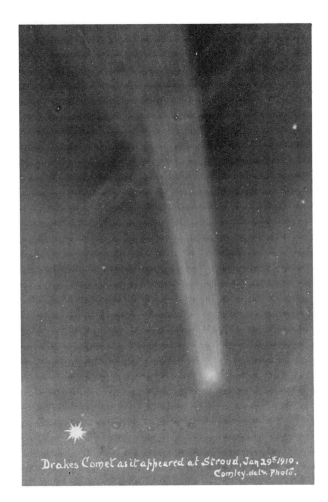

Drakes Comet as it appeared at Stroud, Jan 29th 1910.
Comley.del & Photo.

72. Drakes Comet as it appeared at Stroud on January 29th, 1910, photographed by Comley. Closer examination reveals that it is little more than an artistic impression. Stars never shine as they are portrayed here and the size of the comet itself is enormous. This is a case of the local photographer 'cashing in' on an event by producing a card which he thought the public were looking for.

73. Above: King Street, Stroud. This busy scene in King Street in June 1912 shows a decorated archway built over the roadway for the Agricultural and Horticultural Show. The archway itself depicted agricultural scenes and was built of timber and canvas. Stroud Show continues as an annual event at Stratford Park. The building on the left was the Royal George Hotel and the plate on the wall, F.P. 32.2ft, presumably referred to a Fire Point or Hydrant. The building on the right is Coley the Chemist from where you could obtain Severn Valley Skin Cream or Water Glass for preserving your eggs.

Below: Gloucester Street, in June 1912, looking towards Painswick with another decorated archway. Town Time is on the left and the Greyhound Public House, supplied by Godsells Brewery, is on the right. The street itself shows one of the problems associated with the motive power of the day — horse manure. At the bottom of the hill is one of the culprits hauling a Great Western Railway covered wagon which also states R.T. Smith, Agent. Tucks for Refreshments were Clean and Easy or you could visit the Shaving Saloon or Taylors Cycle Works on the left.

SIR WILLIAM H. MARLING (MARKED WITH A CROSS) AT
THE BONFIRE ON SELSLEY HILL.

74. Left: Sir William H. Marling (marked with a cross) at the bonfire on Selsley Hill. This seems to be a visit by the local gentry to inspect the progress of the work and the opportunity was taken to include the artisans in the photograph for the purposes of good relations. A few local lads climbed the ladder on the right to make sure they were not overlooked. The name Marling survives at present in the form of Marling School. Bonfires of this type were erected with considerable skill and formed part of a chain covering Britain to celebrate Coronations and similar events of national interest. The most recent being the Silver Jubilee of Queen Elizabeth in 1977. This is almost certainly the fire of the Selsley Beacons built by Mr. Edward King for King George V's Coronation in 1911. Sir William Marling died in 1919, aged 84.

Above: Stonehouse. Not all bonfires were erected on the high ground as can be seen by this view at Stonehouse in the Vale but the date of June 1911 celebrates the Coronation of King George V. It was a real occasion for celebration and a good crowd is seen here. The photograph is a wonderful record of dress and expression needing careful examination to be really appreciated. The white collars on the youths' shirts appear to be well starched. Photograph by J.F. Restall of Stonehouse.

75. Selsley Cricket Team 2nd Eleven, photographed by H. Tanner. The motley team could not even produce whites for the occasion but nevertheless the chance to be recorded for posterity was of great importance. It is interesting to note how belts and braces were popular, only to be replaced by trousers with elasticated waistbands in later years. None of the players have a wristwatch but the gentleman on the left has a pocket watch and chain. Hairstyles and moustaches suggest the 1920's.

76. Rodborough Peace Day. Whilst not stating the date, it may have been June 28th, 1919, the date of the signing of the Treaty of Versailles, which may have been a public holiday. A large gathering of the local populace gathered in their best frocks, suits and boater hats to celebrate. As many of the people are facing the same direction, I can only assume they are queuing to enter a hall or church. This type of card is one which would have had a very limited life as it celebrated a particular event. I refer you to the Compiler's Notes in stating that it may well be unique.